CAMBRIDGE

GREENMAN
& THE
MAGIC FOREST

A

Teacher's Resource Book

Marilyn Miller

Karen Elliott

T0349620

Contents

1 Four Rabbits

Follow the sequence and draw.

There are (pegs). / There aren't (doors). (board, computer, window, bag)

Trace and colour.

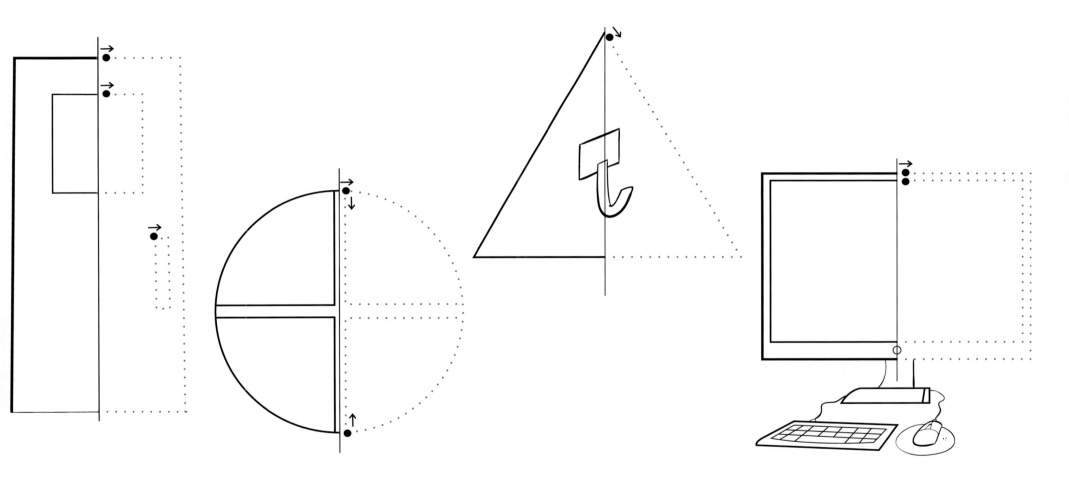

Trace and colour the ants black and the eggs red.

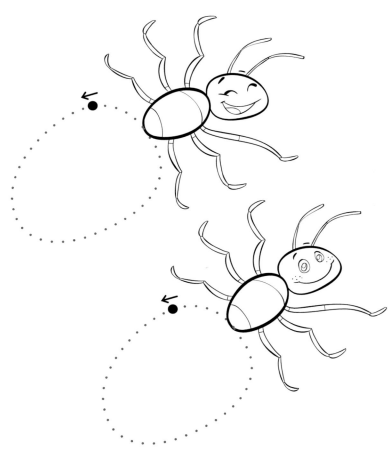

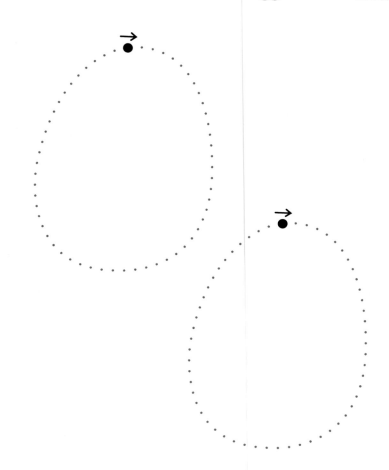

Look and match.

Trace the honey trail.

Help Greenman find the honey.

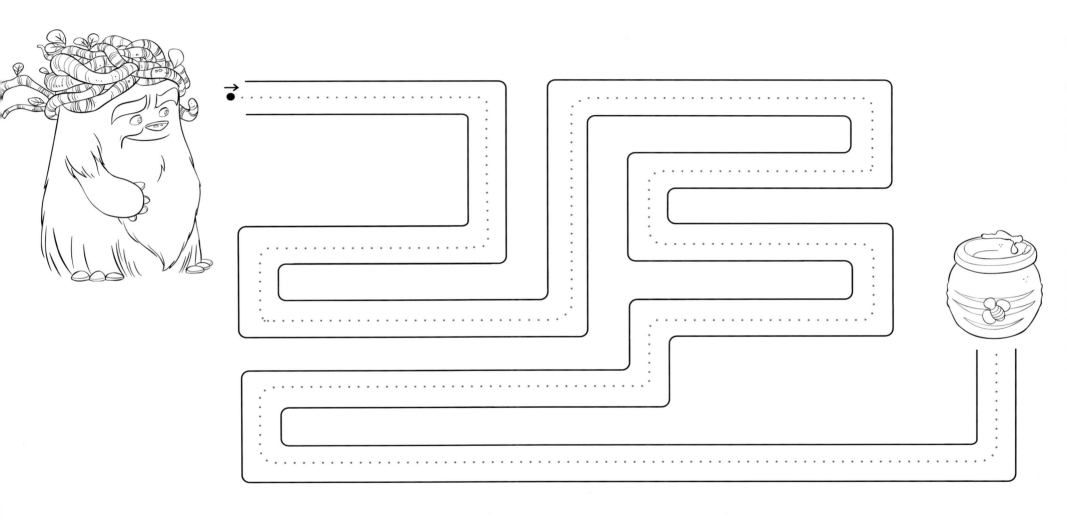

Trace and cut out the insect and the orange.

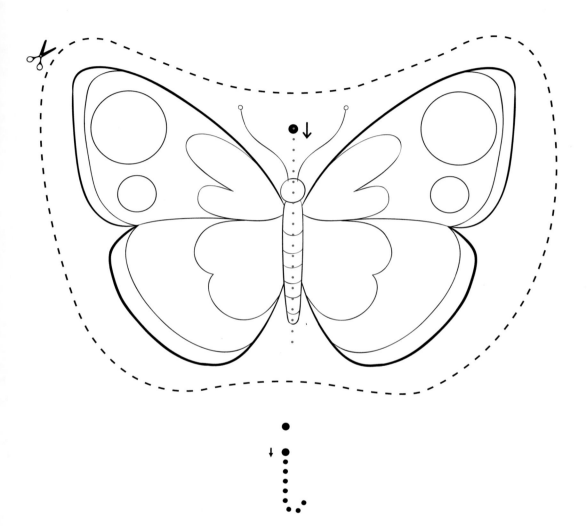

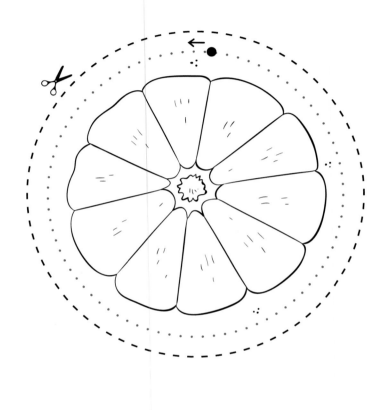

Autumn Fun!

Autumn project: Paint, cut and stick to make a tree.

red, brown, windy, rainy

Greenman and the Magic Forest A © Cambridge University Press. **Photocopiables 9 and 10**

Autumn project: Paint, cut and stick to make a tree.

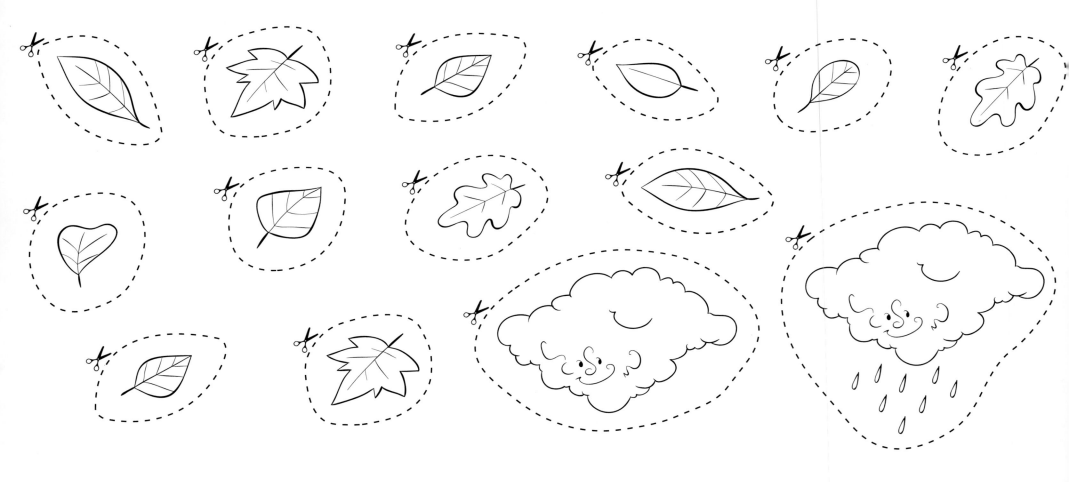

3 I'm Hurt

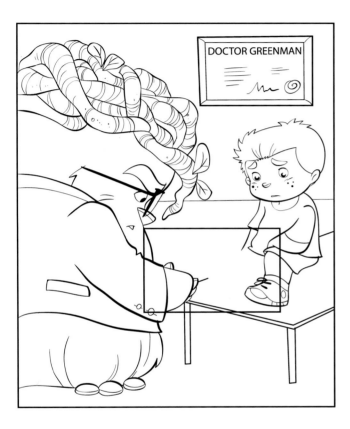

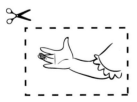

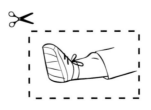

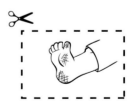

What's the matter? My (leg) hurts. (arm, hand, finger, tummy, foot)

Trace your hand.

Trace the spider's legs. Colour and trace the flower.

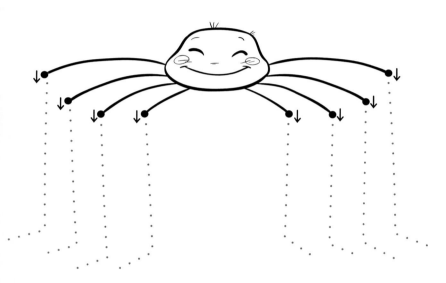

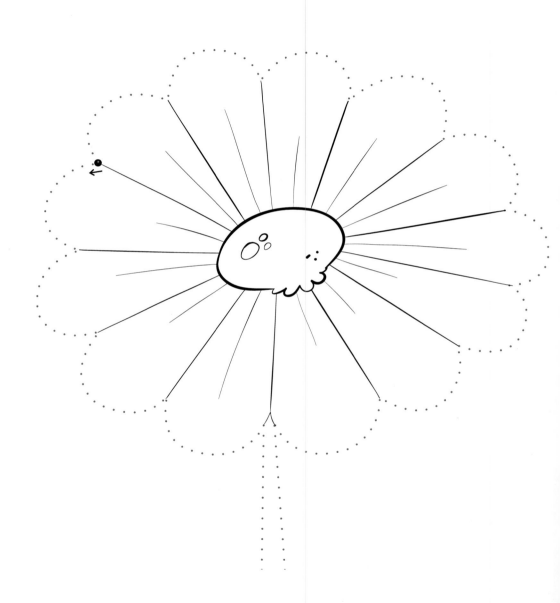

4 It's Too Small

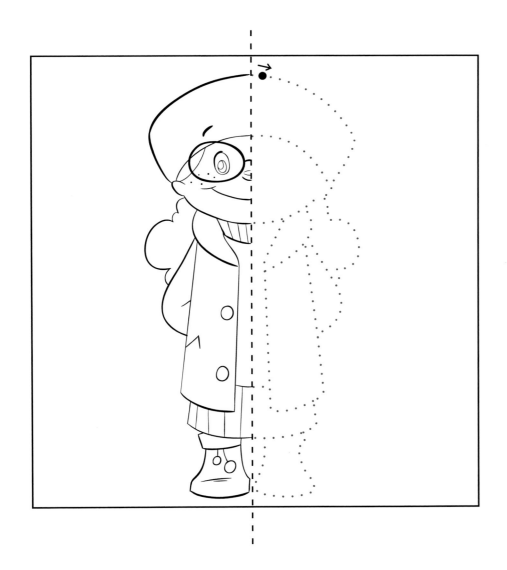

Put on / Take off your (hat). (boots, coat, jumper, dress, trousers)

Cut and stick.

Look and draw.

 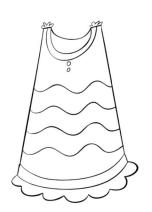  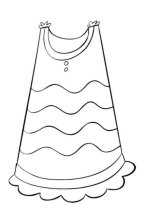 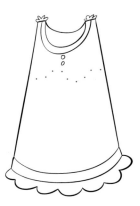

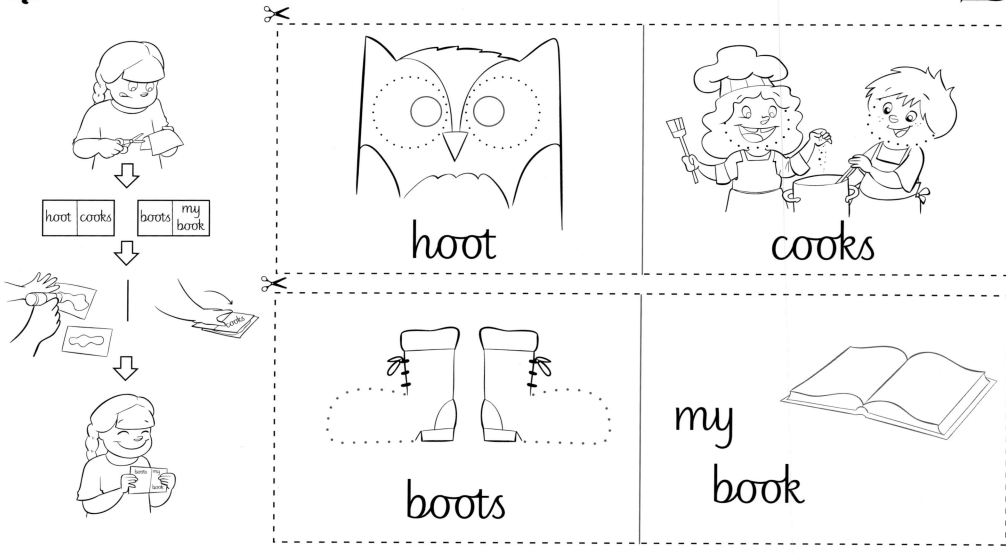

hoot

cooks

boots

my book

hoot | cooks | boots | my book

 # Winter Fun!

Winter project: Paint, cut and stick to make a winter scene.

Winter project: Paint, cut and stick to make a winter scene.

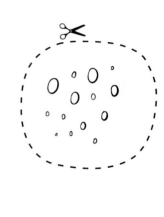

Cut and match.

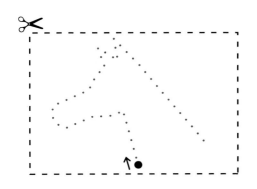

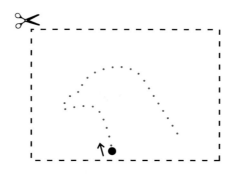

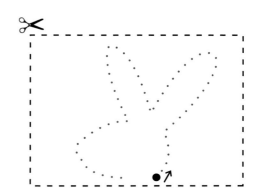

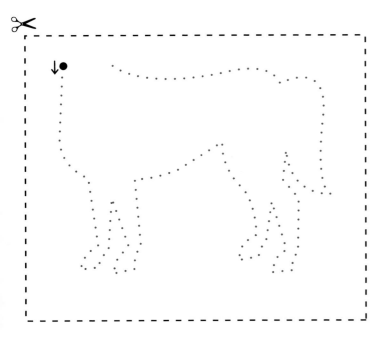

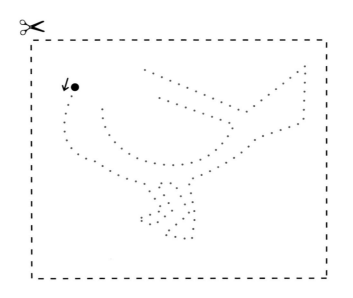

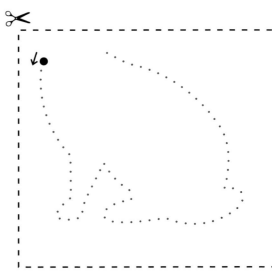

Have you got strong (arms)? (cow, horse, sheep, hen, pig, rabbit)

Circle the strong one.

Value: self-confidence

Trace Hedgehog.

2   3   4

5   6

1

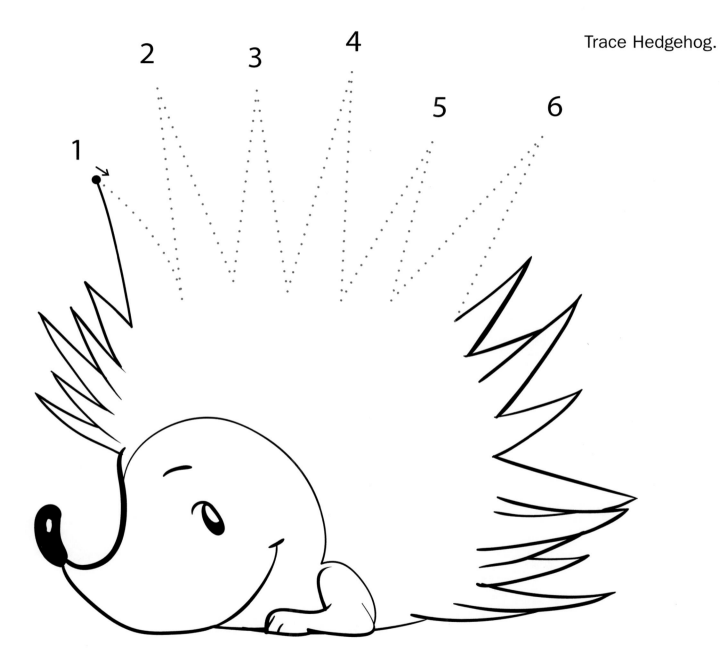

ee   *ee*   *ee*

b____

tr____

sh_p

Phonics: ee (bee, tree, sheep)

6 The Summer Party

Make a food wheel.

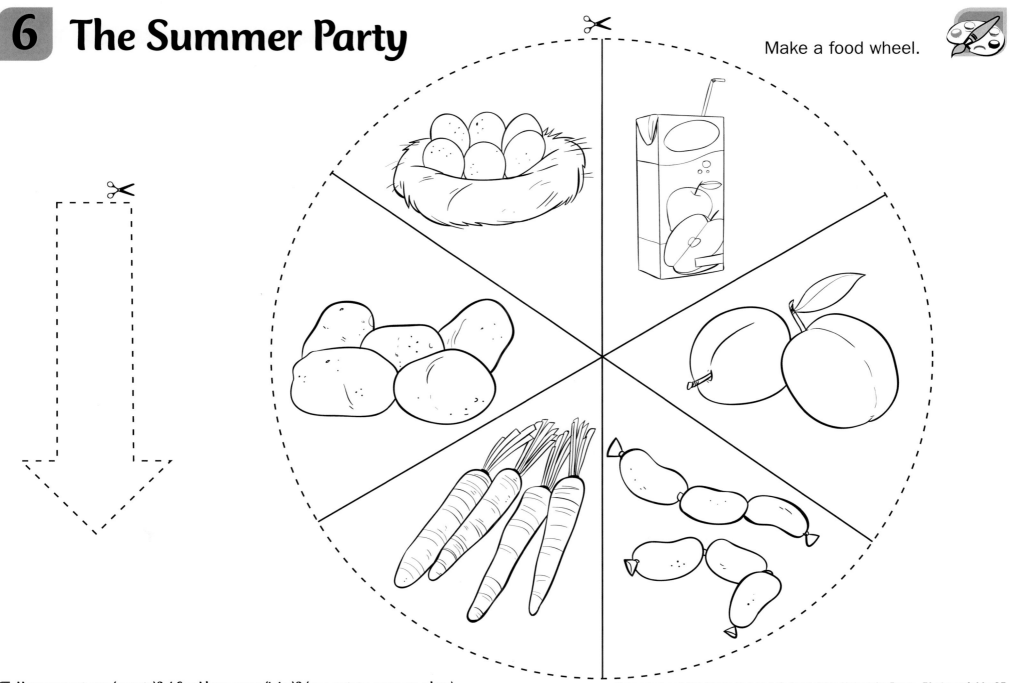

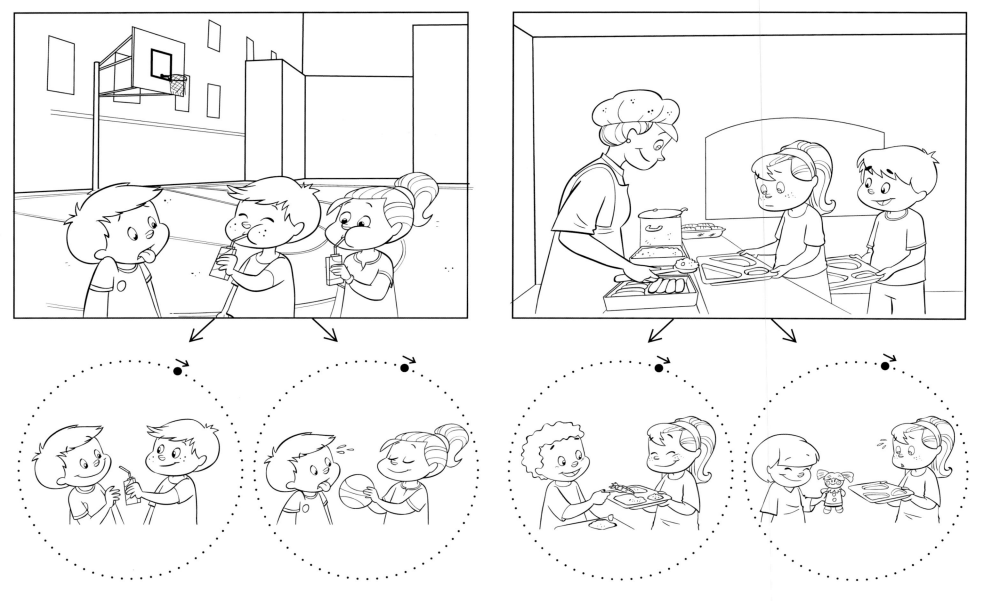

1 ◯

2 ◯

3 ◯

4 ◯

5 ◯

6 ◯

Listen and colour. Then colour by number.

x   x   ng   ng

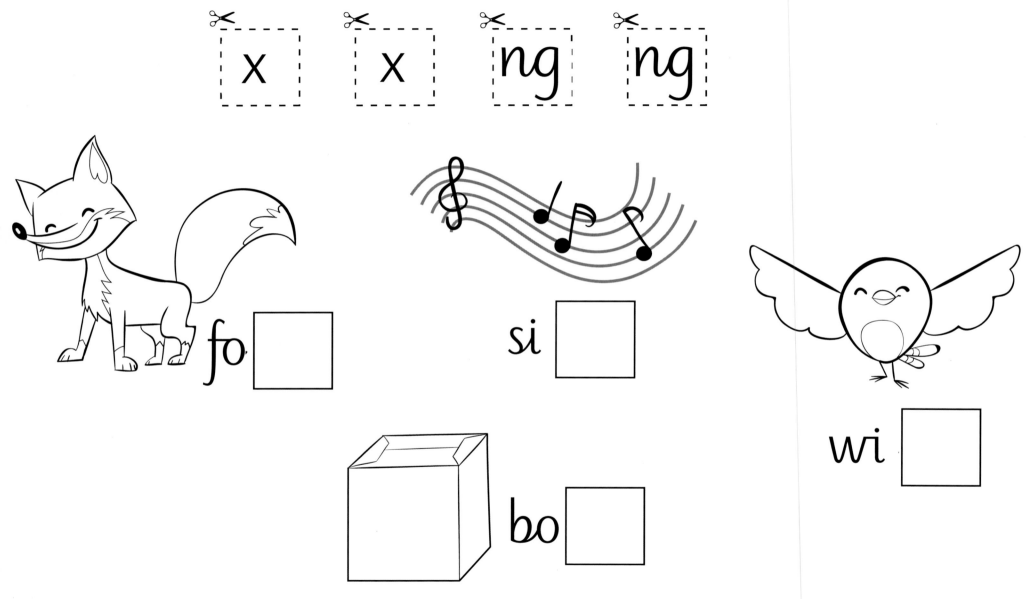

fo☐

si☐

bo☐

wi☐

Phonics: x (fox, box), ng (sing, wing)

Spring Fun!

Spring project: Paint, cut and stick to make a spring string.

green, pink, flower, sunny

Spring project: Paint, cut and stick to make a spring string.

Greenman and the Magic Forest A © Cambridge University Press. **Photocopiables 29 and 30**

Summer Fun!

Summer project: Paint, cut and stick to make a swimming pool scene.

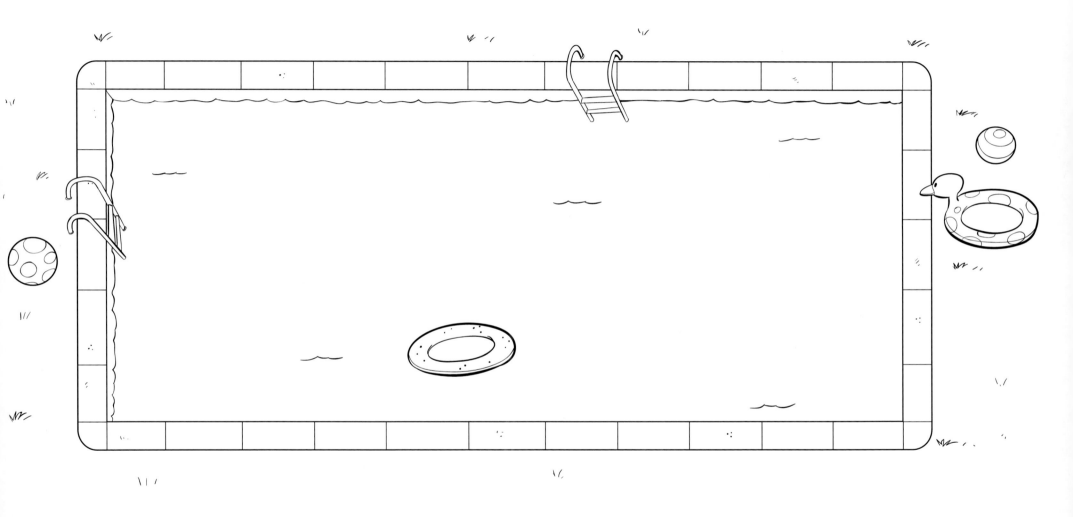

yellow, orange, blue, hot, holiday

Summer project: Paint, cut and stick to make a swimming pool scene.

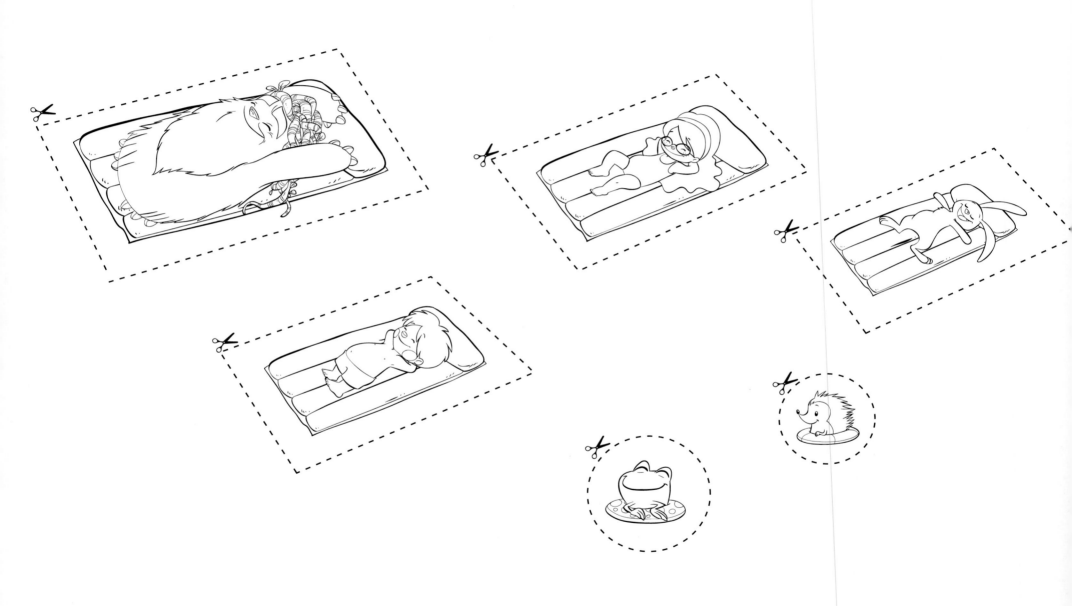

Congratulations!

Name _____

 # Halloween

bat

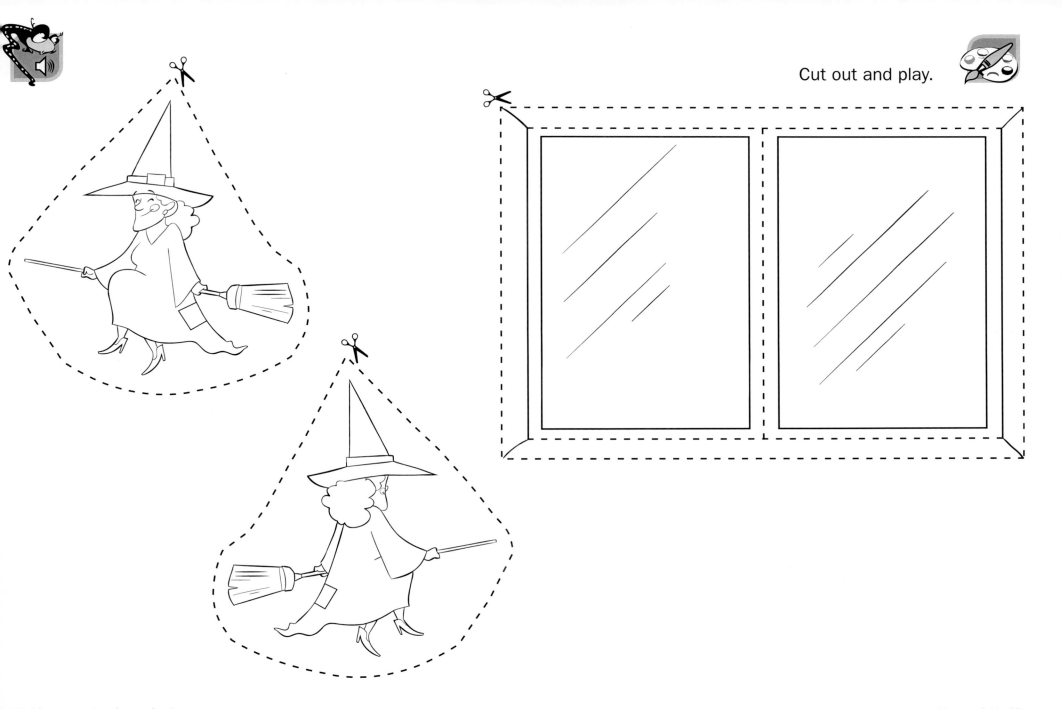

Cut out and play.

 **Christmas**

Trace and colour the Christmas tree.

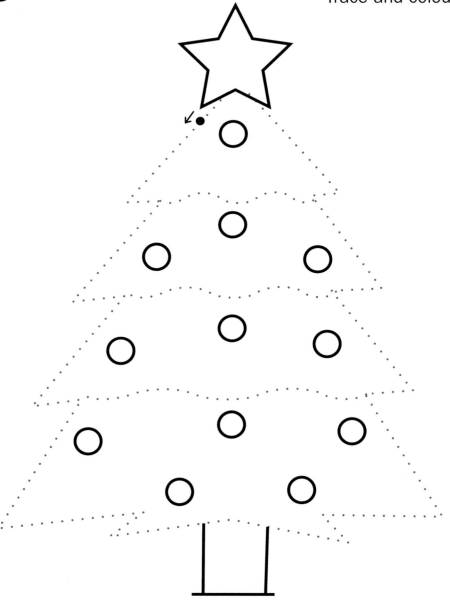

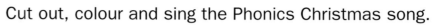
Cut out, colour and sing the Phonics Christmas song.

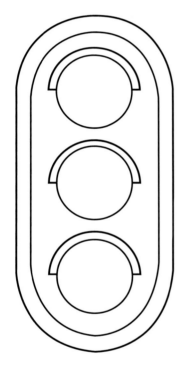

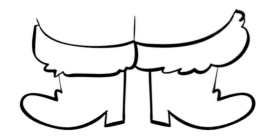

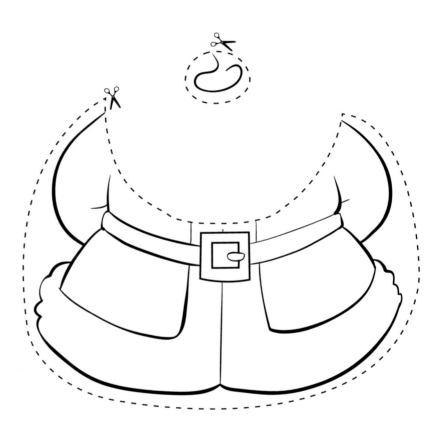

 **Easter**

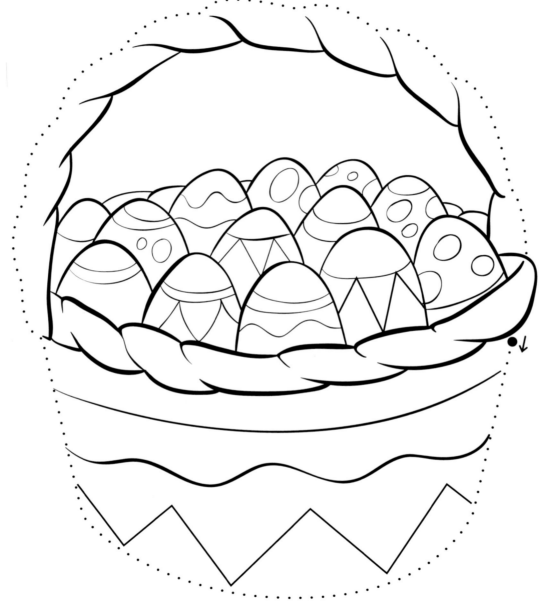

chick, basket

Colour and cut out the chick and the egg. Then sing the Phonics Easter song.

 # Green Day

Help Sam and Nico recycle the rubbish.

help, park, rubbish

Greenman and the Magic Forest A © Cambridge University Press. **Photocopiable 40**

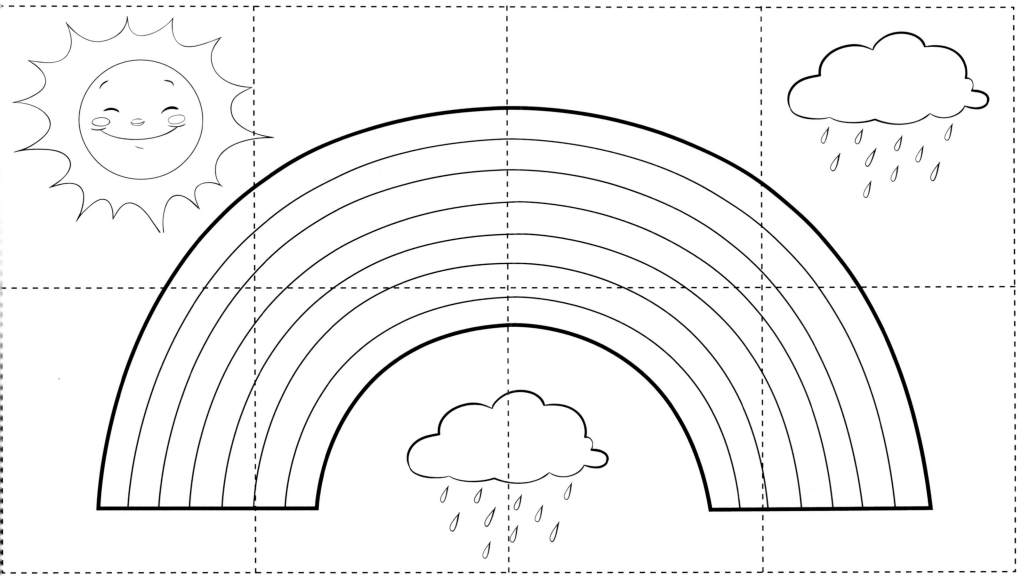

Goodbye!

Goodbye!

Goodbye!

CAMBRIDGE
UNIVERSITY PRESS

University Printing House, Cambridge CB2 8BS, United Kingdom

One Liberty Plaza, 20th Floor, New York, NY 10006, USA

477 Williamstown Road, Port Melbourne, VIC 3207, Australia

314–321, 3rd Floor, Plot 3, Splendor Forum, Jasola District Centre, New Delhi – 110025, India

103 Penang Road, #05-06/07, Visioncrest Commercial, Singapore 238467

José Abascal, 56–1°, 28003 Madrid, Spain

Cambridge University Press is part of the University of Cambridge.

It furthers the University's mission by disseminating knowledge in the pursuit of education, learning and research at the highest international levels of excellence.

www.cambridge.org
© Cambridge University Press 2015

First published 2015

20 19 18 17 16 15

Printed in Spain by Pulmen
Legal deposit: M-3621-2015

ISBN	978-84-9036-829-9	Teacher's Resource Book A
ISBN	978-84-9036-826-8	Big Book A
ISBN	978-84-9036-825-1	Pupil's Book A (with Stickers and Pop-outs)
ISBN	978-84-9036-827-5	Teacher's Book A
ISBN	978-84-9036-828-2	Guía Didáctica A
ISBN	978-84-9036-831-2	Flashcards A
ISBN	978-84-9036-830-5	Phonics Flashcards A
ISBN	978-84-9036-832-9	Class Audio CDs A
ISBN	978-84-9036-833-6	Digital Forest A
ISBN	978-84-9036-845-9	Routine Board
ISBN	978-84-9036-000-2	Reward Stickers
ISBN	978-84-9036-001-9	Reward Stamp
ISBN	978-84-9036-846-6	Teacher's Bag
ISBN	978-84-9036-844-2	Puppet

Thanks and Acknowledgements

Author's thanks

Marilyn Miller would like to thank everyone at Cambridge University Press. In particular, to Jeannine Bogaard and Julieta Hernández for providing me with the opportunity to write, and to Mercedes Lopez de Bergara for her continued support.

Karen Elliott would like to thank everyone at Cambridge University Press and in particular Mercedes López de Bergara for her enthusiasm and dedication to the phonics section of the project; Mary Ockenden at the American School Bilbao, Aitziber Gutiérrez and Piluca Baselga at the Colegio Infantil Haurbaki for their help and suggestions on phonics at various stages of the project.

A special thank you goes to Juan González Cué, our Production Project Manager.

The authors and publishers are grateful to the following illustrators:

Gema García Ingelmo: cover illustration and characters concept
Antonio Cuesta Cornejo: illustration

The publishers are grateful to the following contributors:

Teresa del Arco: layout and design
Chefer: cover design

GREENMAN & THE MAGIC FOREST STARTER
► **GREENMAN & THE MAGIC FOREST A**
GREENMAN & THE MAGIC FOREST B

www.greenmanandthemagicforest.es

CAMBRIDGE
UNIVERSITY PRESS
www.cambridge.org

ISBN 978-84-9036-829

9 788490 368299